Better Than
Throwing Stones

poems by

Jan Ball

Finishing Line Press
Georgetown, Kentucky

Better Than Throwing Stones

ACKNOWLEDGMENTS

Better Than Throwing Stones, *Presa*
Catholic Church in London, *I Wanted to Dance with My Father*, FLP
Novitiate Make-over, *After Hours*
Apologia, *American Poets and Poetry*
Exhalation, *The Lake*, UK
Return to Cloves and Cinnamon, *Children, Churches and Daddys*
Jetlag, *Poets and Artists*
Not a Mandarin, *Poets and Writers*
The Pope in Dorothy's Magic Shoes, *Mad Poet's Review*
Truganini, *Little Brown Poetry*
Barbarian Days, *Immersion Journals*
Breakfast at the Four Seasons, *Open Arts Forum*
Rural Sunday, *BODY, Czech Republic*
English for UAE Students, *Day Job*, FLP
Subbing for Special Ed, *Fine Lines Anthology*
Motherload, *The Magnolia Review*
Outside at Starbucks, *StepAway*
Storybook Daughter, *I Wanted to Dance with My Father*, FLP
The Battle Scars That Soldiers Get, *Halcyon*
Upstate New York Defined, *Indiana Voice Journal*
Why I Collect Netsukes, *Harpy Hybrid*
After Reading Joel Ginsberg, *The Bear Deluxe*
Cross Dressers in Spring Clothing, *Gargoyle*

Publisher: Leah Huete de Maines
Editor: Christen Kincaid
Cover Art: Quentin Ball
Author Photo: Marge Kelly
Cover Design: Elizabeth Maines McCleavy

Order online: www.finishinglinepress.com
also available on amazon.com

Author inquiries and mail orders:
Finishing Line Press
PO Box 1626
Georgetown, Kentucky 40324
USA

Contents

better than throwing stones

"I can throw a stone as far as you can," I say
to my cousin, Bobby, at puny eight, so I throw
a stone at a little boy's head and as I watch
the blood ooze out of his skull like pancake syrup,
his mother comes out on the front porch, her lips
and forehead puckered like a cabbage patch doll,
and asks me conversationally, "Why did you do
that?" but I can only turn my face away in shame
because I'll never know.

I walk the few doors to my cousin's house where
immediately I am rocking in my favorite auntie's
arms as she cradles me the way she'd hold one of
her regular babies while I sob and sob into her pillow
bosom until I have to leave for dinner at my own
house, so I scrape my yellow keds down the Chicago
alley the half-block home as anxious about my mother's
reaction as if I'd lost her one gold, opal ring, yet still
lulled by my aunt's gentle ministrations.

Just past the pink peonies in the side garden, ants
crawling along their serrated petals, I open the screen
door as unobtrusively as possible, but my mother
can see my blotchy cheeks so, stepping aside from
the pork chops she's browning, asks, "What's wrong?"
Eyes rimmed with tears again, I choke out the story
like ejecting a cherry pit half-swallowed, wincing,
half-anticipating the hard slap on my wet cheek I get
accompanied by the shrieked chastisement, "You are
a bad, bad girl."

And I believed her all these years until my daughter
gave me The New York Times best seller: *The History
of Love*, to read where the protagonist also throws
a stone at another child but his father wisely says,
"You'll find something better than throwing stones,"
and I have.

Catholic Church in London

I rest my aching traveler's knees
in the last smooth pew of St. Mary's
Moorfields en route to Marks and
Spencers Finsbury Pavement
(as the British quaintly call some
streets) to buy new monochromatic
socks when I am suddenly jolted
by the ritual I knew as well as
my morning routine of orange
juice, oatmeal, decaffeinated tea—
the deep bass voices of two rows
of clerics wearing white albs
with lacy hoods adoring female
parishioners must have crocheted
by hand resonate like Iris Murdoch's
cursed bell originally must have
sounded as they chant *Agnus Dei*
in the Latin my ears have longed
to hear again and then I register
requiem and know this is a funeral
mass.

Once again, I am lured into a fairy
tale hive of flickering candles, myrrh
and organ music buzzing around me
like the unveiling of the Czestochowa
Black Madonna, music chords as
vibrato as the first *Raiders of the Lost
Ark* sequel beneath the Pankot Palace
or, more germaine, the hypnotic
repetition of the Divine Office I said
five times a day as a Franciscan nun,
intoning, *Oh, God come to my assistance*
at the beginning of each psalm, so,
as the congregation turns toward each
other compassionately for the kiss
of peace, shaking hands or embracing,
I avoid the attempt to communicate
of the woman in the plaid skirt
who briefly catches my eye as if
we're in a poker game: *are you in*

or are you out?

An African acolyte is the only
young male among the graybeards
(I see their bald scalps horseshoed
with sparce white hair from where
I sit adjacent to the action). A man
in tails who must be the funeral
director, appears to ostentatiously
masticate the host as he walks down
the aisle towards me although we
were indoctrinated to think that all
that jaw action was sacrilegious but
maybe that rule has changed as much
as all the others so now it's quite
alright to chew the angel bread.

After I buy the gray socks and an open-
weave green scarf because I hadn't
chosen well before I packed my travel
wardrobe, I need to rest again so I return
to the fragrant old church. The funeral
is gone but there is more chanting
which I realize is the congregation
reciting the rosary. The leader stresses
you in *blessed are you among women*
in a comical way to my ears but no one
giggles: not the celebrant, not
the kneeling people nor miraculously
the statues—The Infant of Prague
in golden cape, as I remembered,
Mary painted in blue, Joseph across
the aisle supportive of his wife and
child as usual, St. Anthony holding
a baby Jesus, or Jesus, Himself,
exposing His bleeding heart above
red flickering vigil lights, not even me.

novitiate make-over

They shuffle into the grand hall, ascetic as hermits
after three days of silence and fasting in retreat then
today the initiation in the almost liquid, lily-fragrant
air of the convent chapel where the choir has been
kneading them like dough with their voices, "O,
Beata Pauperitas", altos holding low notes as steadily
as a hand on the back of a mahogany chair, sopranos
waltzing in the sky as the postulants lay prostrate
on the cold marble floor of the sanctuary, then
the move to the hall, sitting mesmerized, acted upon,
haircut navy style shorter than Steve McQueen's
in Sandpebbles, no more deodorant just talcum
powder with baking soda, no Jean Harlow tweezed
eyebrows, no more brassieres; they have extracted
the white t-shirts and underpants they brought
with them like a trousseau from their trunks
in the furnace room, the cotton undies with legs,
pre-jockey fashionable, the reusable sanitary napkins
that their beloved high school nuns sewed for them
in the paneled convent basement, the two petticoats,
one plaid, one black, wide enough to hide a soldier
like Babushka in Gunther Grass' *Tin Drum*, black habit
on top, white cord with five knots symbolizing Christ's
five wounds around the waist, rosary hung from the side
clattering like wind chimes, a scapular like a long poncho
with the cross symbol of the bride-groom hung on a ribbon
around the neck, black socks and grandma shoes and
then the mystery of headwash: the cap that closes with
straight pins in the back, the stripe that fits under the chin
and clasps on the top of the head with a safety pin
enclosing the face, source of many future headaches,
and finally, the frontlet and veil which someone has
gratefully already arranged so that it fits like a crown,
the veil secured by two more straight pins behind the ears,
their novitiate make-over complete before returning to
the front of the chapel to become engaged to Jesus
in their new clothes.

Vestments

He regularly wears patterned satins
and hand-embroidered albs to say
morning Mass. They shimmer
in the altar lights like a silver fish
in the sun. Once he entones
Go in peace, he walks to the vestry
and changes to his stiffly starched collar
and somber cassock subdued as the black
the rest of us wear: aspirants, postulants,
novices and professed sisters who all
remain kneeling until he leaves the chapel.

This last morning, he steps through the gate
in the communion rail with its white ironed linens
trimmed in lace like a Thanksgiving tablecloth.

His heels click down the two steps
from the sanctuary onto the chapel floor
almost tap-dancing past the first few stations
of the cross on the wall,
including Jesus is Condemned to Die.

We are still adjusting
to our new postulancy routines
and have never seen anyone die,
so only briefly look up
from our meditation books when we hear
the thud of a body collapse on the autumn floor
next to our pews, and hear a guttural scream
intense as a screech owl at night.

His bowels open and evacuate an earthly stench
overwhelming memories of the dignified satin vestments
he wore to elevate the host just a few minutes ago
saying: *This is my body; this is my blood.*

We all thought his body was immortal.

Apologia

I know it's pre-coffee, but the winter sky
is blue; the air is crisp, and I've been reading
Pinker's Language Instinct for an hour,
trying to understand the distinctions in syntax
he makes, wiggling my toes, tapping
my fingertips on my knee, waiting for you
to wake up. The acrobatic chickadees are
having a good time in the holly, and even
the stark, tall honey-locust trees sway
conversationally toward each other in the forest.

So when I heard your slippers on the stairs
and called out, "Let's go to the market,"
I might have curtailed my exuberance
until your brain engaged the day and you
could register the crystal shining air
and the acrobatic chickadees.

book group

Paddy Clark Ha-Ha-Ha at the book group,
a deteriorating marriage while the Irish
sons outwit each other with outrageous
pranks: like Paddy and his naughty Irish
friends dab lighter fluid on the younger
brother's lips, force his teeth apart then
spread it on his tongue and light it.
The mother, apparently oblivious, purple
finger marks above her elbow, feeds
the baby girl and says, "Sinbad, eat your
cereal," Sinbad with scabs on his lips.
My daughter, when I ask her opinion
of the book, e-mails back, "Kids are cruel."
Thank god she missed the point, at least
the point the ladies at the book group made.

International Mail

The mail is slower than the Pony Express;
the card Paul's sister sent from Australia
for our 50th anniversary in May arrives
in July, reliable QANTAS
with the best aviation record in the world
now has a schedule shattered with inactivity
due to Covid 19 travel restrictions,
one more nail in the coffin,
as my parents would have said.

But today, Ros posts photos of pink
and vermillion camellias in her Sydney garden,
and I suddenly feel that I could scurry as fast
as a silvery sand crab across the blonde Gulf
of Mexico beach outside my bedroom window,
rather than slump through another dreary day
reading page after page of David McCullough's,
albeit Pulitzer Prize winning, 900 page Truman.

And more to pack this day like a piñata
stuffed with Licorice All Sorts,
I hear a bi-plane buzz across the sky.

Curious, I walk onto the lanai and see
the plane is pulling a banner that says:
Bellota Will You Marry Me
and I can't stop smiling.

Exhalations

Your exhalations
in my study, where
you sleep
   after your long travels,
make the spiderwort grow
greener on the windowsill;

the cactus blooms
with little blue flowers
when your garlic breath
permeates its spikes and
the mother-in-law tongues
stand straight as Vatican
guards inhaling Italian air.

During the day,
with you gone, I sit
at my desk, mindlessly
shaking the snow globe
you brought back for me
with the *Cathedrale
Sainte-Marie Majeure
de Marseille* trapped
in the middle of a blizzard
I create although I've
only seen the church
in breathless summer.

I know Ile d'if is just
across the bay where
Dumas let his character
almost drown when he
escaped from prison,
gasping for air as he
crawled onto the mainland
rocks exhausted, then later
became the Count of Monte
Christo who exuded lavender
but was venomous with revenge
in every breath he took.

Return to Cloves and Cinnamon

Pomegranates were never enough for you
so I bought mangoes and papayas
inverting the orange mango flesh
into a lattice of three-dimensional cubes
for your breakfast, squeezing limejuice on top,
but you complained when, piercing the fruit with your fork,
you squirted juice on your morning paper.

During the day, after you left for work,
I scooped papaya seeds like tiny eyes
and set them aside to tenderize the dinnerbeef.
Later, I filled the halves with the tenderized meat
then baked them in the oven at 350,
Caribbean style.
The aromatic fragrances clung to the living room walls
and glittered, condensed, on the brittle kitchen windows,
sparkling like contact lenses as the sun set.
I sat on the living room sofa waiting for you
to come home from work,
twiddling my hair, reading PEOPLE magazine.

Where are you now?
The somber moon rises yellow
in a bruised and purple sky,
and I sit alone with the fragrance
of cloves and cinnamon.

jetlag

I'm sitting in London's Hyatt
Churchill waiting for my mixed
green salad to appear; it seems
like hours.

Yesterday, in Lonesome Dove,
the novel I'm reading, Augustus
died. Maybe he died five years
ago for others. Maybe he didn't
die at all since it's just fiction.

Does anyone know what Stephen
Hawkins says about jetlag? Does
anyone know what Einstein said?
Does anyone besides me feel like
they're walking backwards into
a moving London bus when
they're jetlagged?

I see the red double decker buses
come and go, come and go; I
want to say like ladies discussing
Michaelangelo but T.S.Elliot
already said that, still, it is
relevant enough for me to want
to say it fifty years later.

All those old person references
in J. Alfred Prufrock, I never
understood them until recently:
*Do I dare to eat a peach? I have
heard the mermaids singing
on the beach.* I don't think they'll
sing to me, either, anymore.

not a mandarin

Not a mandarin that tasted like
chicken noodle soup, as citrus
connoisseurs describe, nor a kishnu,
sweet tart favorite of many,

I don't know which of the nine
hundred cultivars it was, but
it was the first fruit I'd picked
from a backyard tree except
for apple picking (but that
was in an orchard), the aroma
exploding like Natasha's War
and Peace tangerine fragrance
when she entered the ballroom
toward Pierre,

as I peeled the orange rind, softer
than a navel orange with an almost
acne pit appearance and stripped
the stringy pulp from between
the segments that often get stuck
in your teeth which Mary's mother,
Mrs. Kelly, always said was
the most nutritious part of the fruit
although I suppose that might be
leprechaun lore,

deliciously popping the fresh
crescents into my outdoor mouth
in the gentle Australian winter,
like our Midwest American fall,
spitting the pips on the ground
at the base of the tree trunk, as
Don, having grown up in Sydney,
suggested I do.

The Pope in Dorothy's Magic Shoes

He wears red shoes, so comparisons
with Dorothy seem appropriate. Both
of them iconic, revered, infallible, they
stir audiences to Emerald City expectations,
earlier today, for example, The Stations
of the Cross starting at St. Mary's Cathedral,
attended by the munchkin young congregated
in Sydney for World Youth Week, identifiable
by their orange and yellow backpacks, almost
a costume, and rectangular plastic I.D. tags
located on their chests like a tin man's heart
designating their origins: Mexico, Samoa,
the U.S.—dream destinations for Australian
pilgrims from other parts of Oz, and now
the simulcast Crucifixion across the harbor
from our hotel at the Hungry Mile, purple, red
and white dramatic lights and ecclesiastic music
hanging tonight and all week eerily like menthol
vapor rub between the shores. Technology lifts
the center cross upright with the curly-haired
Jesus actor whose make-up makes him look like
he's been beaten like a victim of police brutality:
he has scrapes and bruises, plus, we see closer
on our tv, he wears a crown of thorns; I know
the story well from my own Catholic childhood.
I shiver uncontrollably like the straw man
in the face of fire, either from the chilly Sydney
night or some primordial memory.

Truganini—The Last Tasmanian Aborigine

You strung my bones
like ivory
for prurient Europeans
to inquire
if I indeed
resembled them
beneath my crenulated skin.

You promised that
my bones would stay intact
unlike my mutilated sisters
chopped in pieces for display
laid out like faceted jewelry.

And now,
The London Times recalls
with pedantry,
"Tasmanian Aborigines
did not completely vanish,"
as if that insect fact
embedded in history
could make the saga golden,
as if our creosoted blood
could ever congeal
into an amber truth.

one more mouse poem

All those cute poems and stories about mice
that make us feel sleepy:

The Field Mouse Came Calling
A Mouse's Telescope
Tiger and Bears in the Mouse's House

and our favorite cartoon characters,
Mickie Mouse and Mighty Mouse

Some of us memorized:
Their tails are long
Their faces small,
They haven't any chins
at all
But I think mice are nice.
By Rose Flyeman

then Gordon pursued one on the sun porch,
last spring
where we had seen it scamper playfully
among the Lincoln Logs
and Fat Brain toys.

When he whacked it with the broom, five foetal
mice flew out of the corpse and
scattered around the room.

Barbarian Days

Again, our shirts and underwear
aspirate lavender fabric softener
with every S. of France breeze
while red geraniums sway
      in their window boxes
on one side of the balcony
     and Mediterranean waves
pulsate on the other.

I sit inside, out of Ianesco's
penetrating sun inhaling
the aroma of peaches
that we bought at the market
Sunday as I read Barbarian
Days and wonder how anyone
would chase waves around
the world as compulsively
as they do in Samoa, Fiji,
Australia or Ethiopia,

yet I can't stay away from here
more than a year.

Breakfast at The Four Seasons

The thin man in the baseball cap who
glides past my table at the hushed 57th
Street Four Seasons Hotel, New York,
looks familiar as he carries his body
like a Limoges vase and I think digitally,
"OMG, it's Kevin Bacon" as he Mystic
River pivots to the farthest corner of
the breakfast room to join a man already
ensconced. My heart vibrates like sitting
courtside during NBA playoffs, and I'm
afraid I'll hyperventilate over my fruit
plate, suddenly faceted citrine pineapple,
chalcedony honeydew melon and Mexican
opal cantaloupe which I sculpt into
the triangles I learned in high school
geometry:
            parallel lines //,
    acute angles >.

The table between Kevin and me is already
occupied by an accountant type accompanied
by a Japanese woman attired stylishly in
a ragged hem jacket patterned in peach
hydrangeas that I admired as they entered
the dining room as if, my dad would say,
they owned it. I don't try to listen to their
conversation but can't help overhearing
when a bull-in-a-china-shop lady joins
them and name-drops *Bob Dylan* twice
and *Rolling Stone Magazine* then loudly
talks about the friends she's kept through
her marriage to her multi-millionaire ($$$)
husband and I wonder why she's saying
this presumably to strangers.

My fruit plate finished, I scatter a few
remaining blueberries and strawberries
around my plate—my version of a surreal
painting—then arrange my fork and fruit
knife handles toward my navel the way
the British and Australians do so I appear

exotic despite my off-the-rack *clothing berlin* pants and top duo. I observe my just-delivered smoked salmon benedict and wonder how I'll ever eat it with these distractions (ADD?)

Furthermore, I wonder what Kevin is eating then realize I must peer at that table for two (2) again, anyway, to reassure myself that my throbbing pulse is justified, so I inconspicuously turn my head like a great blue heron investigating the scent of fish and see the ski-slope nose and deliberate jaw I've admired in *A Few Good Men*, *Flatliners* and tv's *The Following*.

Two new men sit down at the vacated table to my right and I see the one facing me articulate *Kevin Bacon* to his business companion. I catch his eye and slightly nod as sagely as an FBI agent who communicates with a partner incognito under fedora and sunglasses and the man slightly smiles. The clatter of dishes is magnified by my Siemens hearing aids, but I can hear the agent loudly tell the other two about the next drama in her life: the minder they had for their son who got him up for classes at college in California so that they finally attended his graduation last week. I think, *This is beginning to sound like my life.*

By this time, I have picked at my benedict (same name as my high school: St. Benedict Academy although it was only St. Ben's when I went there) poached eggs that have such a small amount of yolk that I wonder

if the chef fashionably added essence
of yolk to genetically modified eggs
to have only albumen since many
egg-white-only dishes on the menu
seem to cater to the chiseled body
shapes I see around me. I nod that I'm
finished to the waiter who could be
a movie star * himself, albeit out of
Bollywood, more like an Indian
Anthony Hopkins in *Remains of
the Day* rather than an action figure
or compassionate army lawyer like Kevin
Bacon. I order one more decaf cappuccino
which I alternate with sparkling water,
no ice, since I always prefer it to tap water,
spooning the foam off the top of the coffee
with a demitasse spoon until my I-phone
shows that my car for the airport has arrived.

Rural Sunday

I see Heathcliff
slink out of the forest
in the morning mist.
He is wearing
a skinny dark suit
like the grackles
in the cornfield.

Cathy has gone
to church
with our neighbors
in Central Illinois
but not me.

I will rise and bank,
rise and bank
in the mist
with the iridescent
grackles
in the cornfield.

I will rise and bank
rise and bank
with Heathcliff
in an iridescent
feathered black suit
and Cathy will
return from church
redeemed and never
die.

None of us will die
on this misty
Sunday morning
in the cornfield.

English for UAE Soldiers

I read bedtime stories
to the Lebron James-
fit-men to demonstrate
how we learn a language.

Stuffed into college desks
designed for slimmer students,
they almost nod off
            like tired children
with the rhythm and
            occasional rhyme
of "once upon a time."

I encourage them to read
to their own children
in bland English
or musical Arabic,
and try to stimulate discussion
asking, "Did your parents read
to you when you were young?"

Yusef, probably the brightest
of the battalion, shares
that his parents were illiterate
yet here he is learning English
at an American university,
he wryly muses.

I taught the soldiers English,
and they taught me how to
kill a man: Just stick two fingers
in the soft space between
his clavicles and push
until he dies.

Was That Stephen King?

A black Bentley gleams where we usually
park our old blue Toyota at the Whitney café
on Longboat Key, Florida, but we don't care:
the sky is Monet blue and the white gravel
crunches underfoot like background sound
in a Hawaiian crime movie as we find
an outdoor table under a palm tree.

Out of the corner of my eye, I see an older man,
my age, in a flamingo pink patterned shirt
who stands up and looks around at the diners,
like he's expecting applause, then takes off
his fedora dramatically and I see he is balding.

I think: *That guy looks like Stephen King* so I ask
my husband, seated across from me, to search
stephen king on his cell. We see the elfish look
of a younger, smiling man with coke bottle glasses
but I can't relate the photos to the man who has left
with two white dogs, one with a black snout like a lion's.

Do lions have black snouts?

When our waitress comes with the seafood platter
we ordered to share I ask her: *Was that guy
in the pink shirt Stephen King?* She says: *I didn't
see him but I'll ask around.*

Meanwhile, a couple approaches us and asks
to share our table. We establish that we all live
on Longboat Key but are snow birds who will soon
be returning to our summer residences in New Jersey
for them and Chicago for us.

I raise the topic of Stephen King and the guy tells us
that the writer moved from Longboat to Casey Key
because an ordinance on Longboat prohibited his dogs
from running on the beach without leashes.
He says that Stephen King is weird (but this guy wears
sunglasses in the shade of the palm tree, himself).

Serotonin sparks in my brain and I ask if the dogs
are two little white ones. He says *yes* at the same time
that another waitress comes to our table and asks:
You wanted to know about Stephen King? He is very weird.
I didn't see him today but he does come here. He wears
very colorful shirts.

Her face glows like Orion when she talks about him.

My aha moment puts two and two together: dogs and shirt,
adds posey behavior, and Bentley probably
for the screen play proceeds for Dolores Claiborne, Misery
and The Shining.

I am convinced that I saw Stephen King.

Subbing for Special Ed

Although I was as American as corn flakes,
the admin still accepted me as a substitute
teacher for English classes at Marrickville
Girls High in Sydney, Australia, before I got
a permanent position.

Absent teachers usually left a quiz or written
assignment but I sometimes added interactive
activities as well, the way I did when I taught
in the inner city of Chicago at Andersen
Educational Vocational Guidance Center
but I'd never taught straight Special Ed,
anywhere, so when I was asked to sub for it
I agreed as reluctantly as if they'd wanted
me to hold a funnel web spider.

The class only had six, but it could have been
twenty-five shop students for how much control
it required. After doing the work the class
teacher had left then as many board activities
as I could think of, I finally gave in and let
the sophomores who had teased me about being
a Hollywood movie star, throw a ball, locking
the door so no one from admin could make
a surprise visit.

The next time I was called to sub for an English class,
I felt confident as the students did group work
on an Aussie book I had read, Randolph Stowe's
A Merry-Go-Round in the Sea. It went as smoothly
as if it had been my own class in Chicago.

I sat in the staff room afterwards relaxing when suddenly
I heard screams. I looked out the glass on the door
and saw one of the Special Ed girls in her blue-checked
uniform running down the corridor screaming:
"I'm not an animal. I'm not an animal."

mother lode

You have always wanted opals from me, gifts
your father gave me, the huge white Australian
opal pendant that you wore for your high school
yearbook photo, still fiery in black and white,
so when I noticed that my little Jamaican
opal earrings were missing, I suspected you
had taken them to India, relieved that they
were not carelessly misplaced but I forgot that
opals are unlucky if they aren't your birthstone
and sure enough you were near the Pakistani
border on September eleventh, the Indian phone
system as noisy as a double drum shearer loader
in a coalmine, Father stranded in Singapore,
himself, urging you to leave Bharatpur or visit
relatives Down Under or at least go south and
me at home, the tv constantly embedding
in my brain both the threat of Muslim extremist
behavior and images of Vikram Seth describing
riots in Indian villages that flare up like stoked
ore furnaces, opalescent, so you finally followed
our advice and headed to Goa on the Portuguese
coast where you said fishermen greeted you
and your new partner, Richard, each morning
with a smile as you emerged from the aqua sea
and in diamond December you came home
and returned the opal earrings to October me.

Outside at Starbucks

London in Chicago this morning,
solo people gravitate toward caffeine
in quilted, black fitted jackets, some
Dickensian bearded, some Martin
Amis clean-shaven, tall women
with dangling earrings, a few
brooding like sad Virginia without
a room of their own.

I sit alone with my decaf grande
carmel macchiata, and write on
the quarto folded description of
the 45,000 mile service my Audi
Quatro will get today on extended
warranty, cell phone on, expecting
a call from the service department
guy just two blocks away.

A man bums a cigarette for a dollar
like a Melville harpooner in a distant
port and I wonder if this is a signal
for a drug deal until I see that the man
who has the cigarettes is joined by
a friend with two cups of steaming
Starbucks which makes me reflect
on what one of our doormen said:
I always carry a cup of coffee to work
at night because a Black man holding
a cup of coffee in a white neighborhood
is not threatening.

Later, when Audi Repair hasn't called,
I struggle to walk home like a listing ship
with my bad knee scheduled for replacement
in February. A woman my age asks, *Are you*
all right? Behind her, a young man briskly
maneuvers from the footpath to the curb
either to be kind or to avoid me.

storybook daughter

You call dutifully as Robin Hood tonight
before I go to bed and the world opens
for me like James and the Giant Peach;
where am I alive if not in the jellied
strawberry layer of your mind, your life
to me like Charlie and the Chocolate
Factory, text-messaging me from a Big
Apple taxi on your way home to off
Houston Street (I'll be sure to pronounce
it right next time) an hour later than me
here in Chicago, mothering you forever
despite your life like a children's book
compared with mine, lately more Violet
Crumbling Bar-yes, an Australian allusion
because, after all, you are half Aussie and
therefore half kangaroo and koala, too, ha-ha.

Where are you tomorrow in your Maurice
Sendak wild island dreams, "Oh please don't
go, we love you so," a family refrain from
your adolescence and sometimes now
(even if your father's love can only peter pan
from far London tonight while I am lonely
here, but I'll never complain as usual, ha-ha);
maybe you're lonely too, but know I love
you alligators all around.

The Battle Scars That Soldiers Get

Not as bad as The Civil War soldiers
that Walt Whitman wrote about
in The Wound Dresser, nor injuries
in WWI that substituted motorized
transport for horses or WWII *triage*
that emphasized *more conservation
of manpower than interests of the wounded,*
according to the British Manual;

Not as bad as the Mobile Army Surgical
Hospital (MASH) that resuscitated units
within 3-12 hours of wounding in Korea
where mortality decreased by 2.4% and
we could see it fictionalized on t.v.
with Alan Alda and Loretta Swit.

Not as bad as in Afghanistan
where improvised explosive devices
detonate when soldiers step on them
causing amputations of toes, legs, fingers,
reconstruction of ankles, but they have
better first aid training now and faster
medivac teams so some soldiers do return
after six months of surgeries and healing.

Bad enough for me, even though my
elective knee replacement heals daily,
two months now since the surgery, but
is quirky, swelling if I walk too much,
sharp pains at random, the worm-like
scar as bas relief as a Diego Rivera fresco
on my right leg when I look at it and think
about all the battle scars that soldiers get.
I know I will heal so I can walk without
a cane again but never back to combat.

Upstate New York Defined

Tonight our didactic waiter in Rosario's
tells us that Rochester is not Upstate New
York but what is upstate if not snow
when our winters there could only have
been more brutal in the Arctic—the snow
accumulating against the garage doors
like fused stalagmites and the adolescents
living with us—our daughter and her red-
haired friend, who we took in when she
told us that her step-father beat her with
a clothes hanger (our daughter had already
called social services), both of the girls
shoveling snow away from the garage
doors with adolescent vigor so we could
hopefully get the Audi out to go to Wegmans
for a prepared chicken as the snow relentlessly
piled half-way up the upstairs windows
like inverted shades, obliterating the pool
house, Karen and Bethany laughing
as joyously as kookaburras, exhilarated
as they shifted shovelfuls of snow into
the red radio flyer wagon then dumped
on the other side of the driveway.

Meanwhile, I holed up in the living room
submerged in Proust in front of the glowing
Vermont wood stove never able to understand
the dynamic interactions: the hormone
shoveled snow, the girl we took in who put
her jeans in the drier so they'd be skin tight,
then had to recline on the bed to zip them,
and our daughter who laughed through
all the storms.

Why I Collect Netsukes

Mine are Japanese Tea-Stained
Scrimshaw Ivory: a miniature
dragonfly on a textured pair
of woven straw flip-flops, signed
Koshido; two tiny amber bees dining
inside a pear; a man seated on a pier
with a fishing pole, signed Shodo;
a scholar; a pumpkin that opens
to show two men playing the board
game, GO.

Already our toddler grandchildren
have tried to pry open the display
case to touch the ridges of the ivory
miniatures, a perfect size for little
fingers to lick and squeeze, but we say,
"No, no," and distract them with toy
trucks.

I wanted a few netsukes after reading
The Hare with the Amber Eyes, Edward
de Waal's memoir about five generations
of his glittering Jewish banking family
whose Austrian property the Nazis
aryanized in 1938 when the servants
opened the cast iron front gates then
fled to make it possible for heavy boots
to echo in the marble halls.

One servant stayed who knew how
the Ephrussi family children were
permitted to cuddle and caress
their choice of netsuke selected
from the collection of 264 pieces
in a black vitrine cherished by Emmy,
their mother, while she dressed for
extravagant Austrian balls or opera,
a gentle time.

Anna secreted the netsukes inside her clothing then hid them in her mattress as she stayed in the house during German occupation while the family fled to London or were interred in concentration camps. Somehow hidden until the war was over, the netsukes passed down through the surviving family, and now Waal's memoir.

Frigate Bird

I am not a frigate bird that flies
two thousand miles without landing,
able to fly so far because I use
only one hemisphere of my brain
to sleep and possibly to navigate
awake with the other one:
                          unihemispheric.

(I don't know if that's just
a technical psych word
              since my computer
has underlined it in red but I love
the sound of it)

I learned about the frigate bird
from an academic dream book
my husband gave me for my birthday
since I have been an avid dreamer

(in REM sleep?)

with vivid nightmares and, in fact,
some wild nights
I have screamed and kicked him.

Now, diagnosed with sleep apnea,
I am connected nightly to a CPAP
machine, (that's an abbreviation)
because the sleep test I took
for Northwestern Hospital
showed that I was waking up about
seventeen times a minute-and
that is considered mild sleep apnea.

Severe sleep apnea, I've learned,
is when you have to exit the expressway
because you're falling asleep while driving.

I rarely kick my husband now and
have not fallen out of bed in a long time
but I see that my poetry colleague
just wrote on Facebook that he has
severe sleep apnea which makes me think
of that frigate bird, hovering
                on the technicolor wind,
awake for hours,
flying high like writing a poem.

After reading Joel Greenberg's
A Natural History of the Chicago Region

Like some adolescent girls, young
"plain pocketbook" mussels click
and clatter their maturing shells
waiting for the right darter, bass,
or sunfish host with scales slicked
back to carry them to other rivers
to colonize. They display their mantles
like dainty purses, minnow-like to attract
the right aggressive species, let him bite,
presuming them a prey, then freeload,
attached to him, as if they're sitting
in the front seat of a Ford Focus,
to richer silt and muck, fortunate
if they do not become bait for bluegills
in their new aquatic habitat.

Research Poem:

Does anyone really want to know about sea slime?

pteropod snails: inflate transparent
bubbles of slime above their coiled
shells like parachutes which keep
them suspended while diatroms,
foraminifers or dinoflagellates
floating along in the sea stick to
their goobubbles overhead so
the snail has a variety of *dishes*
 to choose from for its underwater
Sunday dinner (Prager, p. 33).

Hagfish: is a mega slime-producing
swimmer (picture plate 2) that,
to the poet, resembles a straw mushroom
at one end but would be much less
palatable in Chinese food with all
that protective slime around it. For
shoppers in Korea, the de-slimed black
hagfish skin is used to make handbags,
shoes, wallets or briefcases but buyers
should be cautioned that slime might
re-form on metal attachments so they
might want to carry copious amounts
of hand sanitizer. You never know
(ibid, p. 20).

sea cucumbers: spread mucus-covered
tentacles to accumulate plankton then
transfer the food to their mouths much
as we humans might lick honey off
our fingers (ibid, p. 26).

 University of Chicago Press, 2011

cross-dressers in spring clothing

All night long a doppelganger stumbles naked
from room to room in the conservatory of my mind
parting jungles of hanging vines with yellow, waxy
trumpet flowers, stepping over beaked orange
birds of paradise and intoxicating white lilies streaked
with red veins. When pink morning chases the gray ghost
of my duality away, I dress quickly, take the elevator
down to the still lobby and walk outside to clear my head
but still the world is segmented, the garden cordoned off
with metal railings like sections from a Japanese manga,
comic book panels depicting lewd scenes. This in my
otherwise courteous neighborhood? Purple tulip plants
thrust their compact heads from four inch depths
through the fecund ground like missiles, oblivious to
staring passers-by walking their excited dogs.
And there is no relief from the surreal world of my dreams.
Later in the week the voyeur sunshine peeks between the
erect high-rises where the plants develop more each day
effecting further transformations: gentle flowers opening
out to white stars flushed pink on the outside of their petals,
cross-dressers in spring clothing. As for me, I pour a cup
of tea, submerge myself in Nabokov again but look up
from the page to see a sparkling red kite
released from its controlling rope flying freely in the sky.

www.ingramcontent.com/pod-product-compliance
Lightning Source LLC
Chambersburg PA
CBHW020219090426
42734CB00008B/1138